SERIES TITLES

This Zak Books edition was published in 2009.
Zak Books is an imprint of McRae Books Srl.

THE AGE OF EMPIRE
was created and produced by McRae Books Srl
Via del Salviatino, 1, 50016 – Florence (Italy)
info@mcraebooks.com
www.mcraebooks.com

Publishers: Anne McRae, Marco Nardi
Series Editor: Anne McRae

Author: Anne McRae
Main Illustrations: Francesca D'Ottavi: pp. 13, 24–25,
44–45; Manuela Gaudenzi, pp. 30–31, 34–35, 38–39;
MMcomunicazione (Manuela Cappon, Monica Favilli,
Cecilia Scutti) pp. 26–27
Other illustrations: MMcomunicazione (Manuela
Cappon, Monica Favilli, Cecilia Scutti), Paola Ravaglia,
Studio Stalio (Alessandro Cantucci, Fabiano Fabbrucci,
Magherita Salvadori)
Maps: M. Paola Baldanzi
Photography: Bridgeman Art Library, London: pp. 7tl,
9b, 14c, 17t, 24c, 28bc, 29r, 30t, 36–37b, 39t, 40–41b,
42c, 43c, 43br, 44br; The Art Archive: 11b, 12b,
14–15b, 15t, 15cr, 20c, 23b, 24b, 31t, 32b, 36t, 40c,
42t, 43t; Getty Images: 28t, 33t, 34c, 36c, 37tl, 37tr
Art Director: Marco Nardi
Layouts: Starry Dog Books Ltd
Project Editor: Loredana Agosta
Research: Loredana Agosta
Prepress: Filippo delle Monache, Davide Gasparri
Repro: Litocolor, Florence

Consultants: Barbara Jean Bush is Professor of Imperial
History at the University of Sheffield Hallam, at Sheffield
in the United Kingdom. She has written many articles
and books on slave societies, including *Slave Women in
Caribbean History, 1650–1838* (1990), *Imperialism, Race
and Resistance: Africa and Britain 1919–1945* (1999), and
Imperialism and Postcolonialism (2006).

Library of Congress Cataloging-in-Publication Data

The Age of Empire
 ISBN 9788860981806

2009923554

Printed and bound in Malaysia.

The Age of Empire

Anne McRae

Consultant: Barbara Jean Bush is Professor of Imperial History at the University of
Sheffield Hallam, at Sheffield in the United Kingdom.

Zak
BOOKS

Contents

Indigenous people around the globe paid the highest price of 19th century empire building. In New Zealand, the Maori people, who carved this tiki, lost almost all their land and their way of life to the white settlers.

TIMELINE

	1800	1820	1835	1850
INDIA	Christian missionaries allowed into India.		British Governor General bans traditional Hindu rituals.	Punjab annexed.
SOUTHEAST ASIA	Britain purchases Penang. Raffles founds Singapore.	Java revolt against Dutch.	Sultan of Brunei gives Sarawak to British.	
CHINA	White Lotus rebellion.		First Opium War. Treaty of Nanjing opens up five ports to Western trade.	
JAPAN				Commodore Perry sails into Edo Harbour to open up trade.
LATIN AMERICA	Haiti first country in Latin America to be independent.	Mexico independent. United Provinces of Central America set up.	Most Latin American countries gain independence.	
AUSTRALIA AND NEW ZEALAND	European settlement of New Zealand begins. Governor Lachlan Macquarie adopts name of Australia.		Treaty of Waitangi signed with Maori makes NZ a British colony.	Gold Rush in New South Wales.
AFRICA	Britain acquires Cape Colony.	French invade Algeria. Boers begin the Great Trek.	David Livingstone explores central and southern Africa.	
CULTURAL AND ECONOMIC MILESTONES	Britain abolishes slave trade.	Gold standard established.	Slavery abolished throughout the British Empire.	

Britain built an empire on which "the sun never sank." Queen Victoria, shown here in a statue by a Yoruba artist from Africa, was the monarch who oversaw its creation.

Introduction

During the 19th century European countries greatly expanded their overseas empires. The Industrial Revolution was in full swing in Europe and countries there sought raw materials for their factories just as they were also looking for new markets to sell their products. Famine, poverty, and political revolt, combined with large increases in population, caused a lot of Europeans to look for new homes overseas and many emigrated to places like Australia and Argentina. But while countries such as Britain, France, and Holland were enlarging their empires in Africa, Asia, and the Pacific, Spain and Portugal were losing theirs in Latin America. By 1830 most of the countries in Central and South America had thrown off their colonial overlords. In this book we look at all the various parts of the world during the century that is often called—like this book— "the Age of Empire."

Japan did not succumb to European powers. The menace of colonization caused Japan to modernize and resist Western domination.

1860	1870	1880	1890	1900
Indian Mutiny.	East India Company dissolved. India now run by British government.	Indian National Congress founded.		Muslim League formed in Dhaka.
French capture Saigon.	Dutch attack Aceh sultanate.	France creates Indo-Chinese union.		Spanish-American War. US rules the Philippines.
Taiping rebellion. Second Opium War.			Sino-Japanese War. China loses Taiwan.	Boxer rebellion against foreign interests in China.
	Civil war. Emperor Meiji takes over from shogun.		Japan defeats China in Sino-Japanese War.	Japan defeats Russia in Russo-Japanese War.
Honduras becomes British colony. Jamaica independent.		Costa Rica grants land to Minor C. Keith, founder of Untied Fruit Company.	Cuba independent.	Panama independent.
	Wellington becomes capital of NZ.		New Zealand first country in the world to grant the vote to women.	British colonial rule over Australia ends.
Suez Canal opens.		Scramble for Africa begins. Gold discovered in Transvaal.		Foshoda incident brings Britain and France to the brink of war over Africa.
United States abolishes slavery.	Frozen meat shipped from Argentina.	Brazil abolishes slavery.		

Right: Poster advertising chocolate made from cocoa imported from the colonies.

Fry's Cocoa Pure Concentrated **AND MILK CHOCOLATE**

Markets and Materials

There were many reasons why the imperial powers were interested in expanding their empires. One was strategic: to keep their rivals from becoming too powerful. Another was to increase trade. As Western powers industrialized, they needed to look further afield for raw materials and markets. Many of the colonies had excellent climates for growing products such as sugar, tea, coffee, fruit, and cocoa, and were rich in natural resources.

Afghans Resist Britain

During the late 19th century, both Britain and Russia wanted to control Afghanistan. The competition between the two imperial powers was called the Great Game and resulted in two wars: the First Anglo-Afghan War of 1839–42 and the Second Anglo-Afghan War of 1878–80. The Afghan tribesmen, who were fiercely independent, managed to resist the British, and the British finally signed a border agreement and an agreement to recognize Afghanistan's independence. Afghanistan became a buffer between the British and Russian empires.

Afridis tribesmen from Afghanistan, who showed fierce resistance to the British.

Japanese Colonialism

By adopting Western-style government, military, and technology, Japan was able to avoid colonization and become a major colonial power itself. Successful wars against China 1894–95 and Russia 1904–05 resulted in Japan gaining control of Korea, Taiwan, southern Manchuria, and half of Sakhalin.

Colonialism

Colonialism is the extension of a nation's government over territory beyond its borders. Colonial powers either send settlers to take over the colony, or set up a local government to exploit the indigenous people and their wealth. During the 19th century several European countries built up such vast overseas colonies that they were called empires. Britain, for example, gained power over a quarter of the world's land surface and controlled roughly the same percentage of the world's population. France, Germany, Italy, Belgium, Portugal, as well as the United States and Japan claimed territories across the world. Although the imperial powers developed many of their colonies, bringing international trade and infrastructure (railroads, for example), the colonists often treated indigenous peoples badly, seizing their land and depriving them of some of their most basic human rights.

Emperor Meiji came to power in 1868. He modernized Japan, preparing its path to become a world power.

THE PEAK OF EMPIRE 1912

CANADA

UNITED STATES OF AMERICA

BRITAIN

RUSSIA

CHINA

JAPAN

INDIA

AUSTRALIA

- British
- French
- German
- Italian
- Russian
- Dutch
- Portuguese
- Japanese
- Spanish
- Belgian
- American
- Danish

A European Free For All

From 1870 European powers rushed to expand their empires. During this time two major continents, Africa and Asia, were almost completely carved up. Missionaries, traders, and military officers all saw enormous potential in these areas and pressed their countries for imperial advances. Britain and France, as well as emerging powers such as Germany and Italy, concerned about the strategic advances of their rivals, scrambled to seize new territories. They also raced to claim areas rich in natural resources for the new wave of industrialization. Britain made the largest additions to its empire during this time, seizing lands all over Africa as well as strategic points in the Pacific.

Map showing the British Empire in about 1886.

"Anglobalization"

In 1897, in the year of her Diamond Jubilee, Queen Victoria of Great Britain reigned over the largest empire the world has ever seen. The British Empire was three times larger than the French Empire and ten times larger than the German Empire. Some 445 million people lived under some form of British rule. Britain led the scramble for Africa, as well as gobbling up huge territories in Asia and Oceania.

The Scramble for Africa

After British explorers traveled inland in Africa, claiming new areas for the queen, Britain began to colonize vast areas of the continent. Between 1880 and 1914 the British gained Egypt, the Sudan, Uganda, Kenya, Nigeria, and Northern and Southern Rhodesia. They also consolidated their rule of South Africa with their victory in the Second Boer War of 1899–1902.

This cartoon of British statesman and businessman Cecil Rhodes (1853–1902), shows his desire to see Britain bestriding Africa. Rhodes made a fortune in the diamond industry. Rhodesia (now Zambia and Zimbabwe) was named after him.

Right: In Indochina a group called the Black Flags, led by De Tham(top right), resisted French domination.

In this cartoon an evil serpent, symbolizing imperialist Britain, squeezes the globe, squashing traditional cultures.

European Explorers

European explorers traveled extensively in Africa before it was colonized. On returning to Europe, many encouraged their governments to begin colonization. In the words of British-American explorer Henry Morton Stanley, it was their duty "to put the civilization of Europe into the barbarism of Africa."

Asia gets Carved Up

Britain controlled the Indian subcontinent, Burma, Malaysia, Singapore and many other parts of Southeast Asia. The French gradually took over Indo-China, while the Dutch maintained their extensive empire in Southeast Asia, or the East Indies, as the region was known then.

Left: French explorer Count Pierre Savorgnan de Brazza sold photographs of himself to help finance expeditions north of the Congo River in the 1880s.

India and the East India Company

After the British East India Company virtually annexed the state of Bengal in 1765, it began to change from a trading company into a military and political institution. In the India Act of 1784 the British government had declared that territorial expansion was against "the honor and policy of this nation." However, territorial expansion did occur, and by the middle of the 19th century the British effectively ruled India. Early governors believed that British rule would be brief. Then the idea arose that their rule was a great benefit to the Indian people, a "sacred trust." At first the British treated Indians as equals and did not interfere with local customs, but once the "sacred trust" idea took hold, they began to enforce reforms, many of which were strongly resented by many groups of Indians.

Ram Mohun Roy (1772–1833) was a Hindu liberal reformer who opposed the caste system and adopted aspects of Christianity. He founded the Brahmo Samaj (Society of God, 1828) and the Hindu College in Kolkata (Calcutta) (1817), and had great influence on the British as well as Hindus.

Hindu Reformers
The British could not have ruled India without the co-operation, active or passive, of most Indians. While Muslims in general kept themselves apart from Western influences, a growing number of Hindus identified with them. They spoke English (the official language) and studied European history and literature. Many government reforms were brought about by pressure from Hindus.

Before a bridge was built, this locomotive was ferried across the Indus River.

Making block-printed cotton cloth. The collapse of India's cotton trade brought severe hardship.

Roads and Transportation
No roads existed in India before 1830. The famous Grand Trunk Road between Kolkata (Calcutta) and Delhi was begun in 1839. The first railroad was constructed from Bombay in 1853. The British governor-general's plan was to develop trade routes connecting the seaports of Mumbai (Bombay), Kolkata, and Chennai (Madras). This involved tremendous feats of civil engineering, including crossing mountain ranges and the great Ganges and Indus rivers. Nearly 40,000 miles (70,000 km) of railroad track were working by 1914.

The British
In the early days, many of those employed by the East India Company retired to England with huge fortunes. This profiteering was later stopped, but life in India, though it had drawbacks, was very comfortable for the ruling British. A young nobody in London, sent out as a clerk for the Company, found himself with a large house and 20 servants. Some Britons came to love and understand Indian ways and chose to stay on after retirement, but others were bored, superior, and increasingly racist.

Right: A "memsahib" (meaning "the lady of a sahib," a man of high status) with her servants.

Trade and Industry
The British saw India as a market for its booming industry and did not invest in Indian industry, which might compete. The Industrial Revolution was a disaster for India's cotton workers (as it had been earlier for Britain's own hand-weavers). Hindu ritual and the caste system also hindered technological progress. However, India was brought into the world capitalist system, with great benefits for the merchants and bankers of the growing middle classes, who became closely identified with British rule.

The Princely States

One third of British India was made up of nominally independent states. The British recognized the value of maintaining the Indian princedoms, and until 1858 many areas experienced little contact with Europeans. But British reluctance to interfere was combined with reforming zeal. The custom of killing baby girls, for example, was unacceptable, so the British made it a capital crime, yet failed to end it entirely. After 1858, under the rule of the Crown, the princes felt more secure. They generally remained firm allies of Britain.

Below: Procession with Maratha ruler Serfoji II, Rajah of Tanjore in southern India from 1787. Soon after gaining power, he was deposed by his uncle and regent Amarsingh who seized the throne for himself. With the help of the British, Serfoji recovered the throne in 1798. A subsequent treaty forced him to hand over real power in the kingdom to the British East India Company. Serfoji remained until 1832.

Territorial Expansion

In 1780 the British were confronted with three major enemies: the Marathas, the Nizam of Hyderabad, and Tipu Sultan of Mysore. It took three wars to defeat the Marathas and establish British supremacy, while other campaigns resulted in British authority stretching, in the east, from Bengal to Sri Lanka (Ceylon). Other states were taken over when the ruler died without –according to the British, but not Hindu, interpretation–leaving a direct heir.

After the death of Ranjit Singh (1839), the Punjab fell into disorder. Invasion of British territory resulted in war and annexation under Ranjit's successor, Duleep Singh (left).

INDIA 1784–1857

1784
The India Act says British will not expand further.

1798
Ceylon (modern Sri Lanka) becomes British colony.

1799
Tipu Sultan is defeated by British Governor General Cornwallis and killed.

1813
Christian missionaries are allowed to preach in India.

1815
Around 40 million Indians under British rule.

1818
Final defeat of Marathas.

1828–35
British Governor General Bentinck bans traditional Hindu rituals, including suttee, thuggee, and infanticide.

1835
English becomes the official language in schools in India.

1836
Large road-building program begins.

1839–42
First Afghan War. Ends with humiliating British defeat.

1849
Punjab annexed.

1853
First railroad in operation.

1856
Oudh annexed.

India after the Mutiny

Increasing hostility to British rule led to a widespread rebellion, known as the Indian Mutiny, across north and central India in 1857–8. It took 14 months of bitter fighting to put it down. At the end of the rebellion the British government took over from the East India Company, and from that point on India was governed by a tiny minority of British civil servants. The Indians, forbidden to participate in the government of their own country, began to organize themselves to regain their independence.

BRITISH INDIA 1914

AFGHANISTAN · KASHMIR · PUNJAB · TIBET · CHINA · DELHI · NEPAL · MEWAR · SIND · BENGAL · ASSAM · OUDH · CALCUTTA · BURMA · BOMBAY · ORISSA · ARABIAN SEA · HYDERABAD · BAY OF BENGAL · GOA · MADRAS · MYSORE · CEYLON

◻ Possessions 1858   ◻ Acquired 1858–1914   ◻ Dependent Indian states

British Territories and Spheres of Influence
By 1914 Britain effectively controlled the entire Indian subcontinent, either by direct rule or through the rule of dependent princely states and protectorates. Beyond India, they gradually took over Burma to the east. In the west, they failed to absorb Afghanistan into the Indian Empire. Fierce Afghani tribesmen repelled the British twice and Afghanistan remained an independent buffer between the British and Russian empires.

The Mutiny

New practises introduced in the army offended the Company's Indian soldiers (called "sepoys"), both Hindu and Muslim. In 1857 several regiments mutinied against their British officers. The rebellion spread across much of northern India, fuelled by hostility to British rule. Delhi was captured and fighting was fierce (above). Horrible atrocities were committed by both sides. The Mutiny was ruthlessly crushed in 1858; many civilians were executed without trial.

Meaning of the Mutiny

The rebellion was more than a mutiny, but it was not a nationalist rising. Few Indians yet thought of an all-Indian "nation," and no great leader emerged to unite resistance to the British. The motives of the rebels were conservative. They feared that modernization was destroying their ancient culture.

Left: Rebel sepoys from Bengal.

Law and Administration

In theory, Indians were to be part of the civil service that ruled India after the mutiny but in practise hardly any Indians were recruited. Often, an inexperienced British district officer would be in charge of an area containing a million people. Excluded from the administration of their own country, many Indians turned to nationalism.

The End of East India Company Rule

The mutiny ended the rule of the East India Company. After 1858 India was placed directly under the British government, with a viceroy and a council, responsible to the government in London. Indian involvement in government was increased by later acts, but the concessions were minor (though resented by many British).

Left: British officer ruling over a court in the Punjab.

Below: British Queen Victoria was crowned Empress of India in 1876.

Famine

Famine was a continual curse in India. It could wipe out half the people in a town or region. Relief usually arrived too late. The 1866 famine in Bengal, with over a million dead, was made worse by monsoon rain preventing transportation and merchants hoarding grain. In 1883 the government set up an elaborate plan, the Famine Code, to deal with the problem. It was an unusually large social-welfare program for the time, and brought improvement, but did not stop famines.

The National Congress and the Muslim League

The Indian National Congress was founded by educated Hindus and Muslims in 1885. Its original object was to press the government for a greater share of power for Indians; national independence was not part of the agenda. A more extreme wing soon emerged and gained control of the party. It advocated self-government for India as a dominion of the British Empire, like Canada or Australia. Muslims in the Congress feared that, in a more democratic India, they would be swamped by the Hindu majority. They founded the separate Muslim League in 1906, which reached an agreement with Congress (the Lucknow Pact) for certain seats to be reserved for Muslims in future elections. Members of the League took part in the non-cooperation movement and some Muslims remained members of Congress.

Right: B. G. Tilak (1856–1920) led the extreme wing of Congress. He first had the idea of opposing the British by massive civil disobedience, or non-cooperation, the policy later adopted by Gandhi.

Below: The Delhi Durbar was a large assembly held at Delhi to celebrate the coronation of a new British king or queen (who were also emperor and empress of India). The Delhi Durbar of 1903 included two weeks of dazzling celebrations planned by British Governor General Lord Curzon. King Edward VII and Queen Alexandra did not attend.

Indo-China

French traders and missionaries had been interested in Indo-China since the 17th century, but it wasn't until Napoleon III's troops captured Saigon in 1858–59 that French influence took hold in the region. From the 1820s the British gradually took control of the western half of mainland Southeast Asia, including the Malay Peninsula. Siam (modern Thailand) lay between the French- and British-controlled territories, creating a buffer and never becoming a colony itself.

The Malay Peninsula

Britain gradually colonized the Malay Peninsula, beginning with the purchase of the island of Penang in 1796. British Malaya was never united under a single administration; even so, as the world's largest producer of tin and rubber, it was one of the most profitable of British colonies.

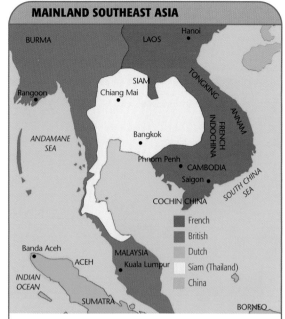

Right: Detail of a Burmese painting showing the royal elephant carrying the king in an elaborate enclosed basket.

French Indo-China

The French fought long and hard to gain control of Indo-China. During the Tonkin campaign (right), they battled against the Vietnamese and various Chinese armies. Like the other European powers in the region, the French wanted access to valuable local produce, including rubber, rice, silk, and tea. They concentrated on modernizing their colonies and maximizing profits. Peasants were encouraged to sell their land and take jobs in the salt mines or opium factories.

MAINLAND SOUTHEAST ASIA

The British and French in Mainland Southeast Asia
To protect India's borders, Britain annexed Burma in three separate wars between 1824 and 1886. Burma was administered as part of British India. The French captured Saigon in 1858–59 and then gradually acquired other territories. By 1887, after several years of undeclared war against China, they had successfully merged Cochin China, Cambodia, Annam, and Tongking into the Indo-Chinese Union. Laos was added in 1893.

Thailand

Thailand, known as Siam, was ruled by the Chakri Dynasty of kings in the 19th century. The first Chakri king, Rama I (reigned 1782–1809), moved the capital to Bangkok in 1782. He and his successors became increasingly worried as they saw neighboring countries being absorbed into European empires. However, they were able rulers and by studying English and learning European ways were able to keep their country independent.

Below: Rama IV (reigned 1851–68) was interested in astronomy. In 1868 he correctly predicted an eclipse of the sun and invited his doubting courtiers and members of the foreign community in Bangkok to accompany him to Sam Roi Yod to view the eclipse.

Island Southeast Asia

By 1890 all the islands of Southeast Asia were under European rule. The Dutch East Indies covered almost all of what is now Indonesia, the Spanish controlled the Philippines, the British had Sarawak, Brunei, Borneo, and Papua (as well as Singapore), while the Germans and Portuguese held German New Guinea and East Timor, respectively. The Europeans met with fierce resistance as local rulers sought to protect their valuable lands and exports. Nationalist movements gathered force and there were frequent uprisings.

Below: A Wayang shadow puppet from Indonesia. Traditional culture was not strongly affected by Dutch rule.

Right: Raffles realized immediately that Singapore, with its deep natural harbor, abundant supplies of fresh water and timber, plus its position near the Straits of Malacca was exactly what he needed.

The Dutch

The Dutch consolidated their hold on fertile Java in the bitterly fought Java War of 1825–30. Dutch colonial authority rested on a tiny percentage of the overall population—there were just 42,000 Dutch troops and armed police to rule over a combined population of 62 million in Indonesia.

Singapore

Sir Stamford Raffles landed at Singapore in 1819. He negotiated a treaty with a local leader to develop the southern part of the island for the British East India Company. A free port was established which attracted Chinese, Arab, and Malay traders who were happy to avoid local Dutch levies. The settlement grew rapidly and the whole island became a British colony in 1824. Although the Dutch government protested, Singapore remained a British colony and continued to flourish throughout the 19th century.

Below: A view of Singapore from Government Hill in 1830.

ISLAND SOUTHEAST ASIA 1800–1900

1811
Dutch give up Java to British invasion.

1814–16
Dutch regain Java.

1819
British administrator Sir Stamford Raffles founds Singapore.

1825–30
Revolt against Dutch rule of Java.

1841
Sultan of Brunei gives Sarawak to the British to repay help in putting down rebellion.

1859
Dutch and Portuguese agree to partition island of Timor.

1873
Dutch attack the Aceh sultanate.

1884
Germany annexes northern New Guinea and the Bismarck Archipelago. Southern part of the island to Britain.

1898–99
Spanish-American War. The US take control of the Philippines.

Above: An American soldier sitting on a church statue during the Spanish-American War of 1898.

The Spanish in the Philippines

The Philippines had been a Spanish colony since the 16th century. The archipelago was administered from Mexico until 1821 and then directly from Madrid. The Spanish built towns, introduced new crops and livestock, and encouraged trade. Missionaries converted the population to Christianity and founded schools, universities, and hospitals. In 1896 a revolution against Spain ended with the establishment of the First Philippine Republic. However, the Treaty of Paris, at the end of the Spanish-American War, gave control of the Philippines to the United States.

Valuable Trade

Southeast Asia had been a sources of spices for European traders for centuries. At the end of the 19th century, rubber began to be commercially grown in Malaya and Indonesia from plants imported from South America. Rubber became an important crop, along with traditional exports such as rice, tin, copra, and oil.

Right: Indigenous peoples of New Guinea photographed in 1885 by a Danish explorer.

New Colonial Players

Germany was slow in developing its colonial interests in Southeast Asia but in 1884 it laid claim to the eastern part of the island of New Guinea. It was partly blocked by Australia, and then Britain, and its presence was limited to the northern part of New Guinea and the Bismarck Archipelago.

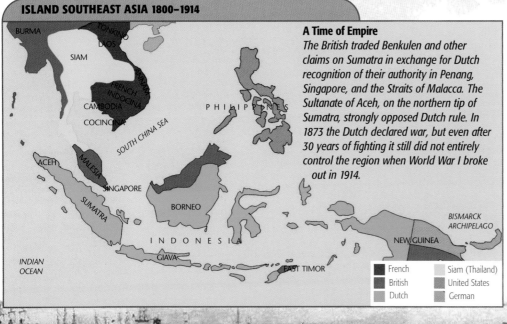

ISLAND SOUTHEAST ASIA 1800–1914

BURMA
TONKING
LAOS
SIAM
ANNAM
FRENCH INDOCHINA
CAMBODIA
COCINCINA
SOUTH CHINA SEA
PHILIPPINES
ACEH
MALESIA
SINGAPORE
SUMATRA
BORNEO
INDONESIA
GIAVA
EAST TIMOR
BISMARCK ARCHIPELAGO
NEW GUINEA
INDIAN OCEAN

French | Siam (Thailand)
British | United States
Dutch | German

A Time of Empire

The British traded Benkulen and other claims on Sumatra in exchange for Dutch recognition of their authority in Penang, Singapore, and the Straits of Malacca. The Sultanate of Aceh, on the northern tip of Sumatra, strongly opposed Dutch rule. In 1873 the Dutch declared war, but even after 30 years of fighting it still did not entirely control the region when World War I broke out in 1914.

China

China had enjoyed a long period of prosperity and growth under its Manchu rulers in the 18th century. The emperor Qianlong reigned for 60 years, abdicating in 1796 in order not to rule longer than his grandfather, Kangxi. In contrast, the 19th century would prove to be much more difficult. Despite efforts to keep them out, "barbarian" Western traders and businessmen gained ever larger footholds in China. British imports of opium from India led to two so-called Opium Wars. China lost both wars and was forced to concede even more trading rights to Western powers. To add to their problems, the Manchu also had to deal with internal corruption, high taxation, and frequent rebellions.

A painted fan decorated with a scene of Guangzhou, where the flags of different European trading nations are flying.

The Opium Wars

To stop the outflow of silver, which the Chinese paid to traders in return for opium smuggled in from India, and to fight the spread of drug addiction, in 1800 the Chinese banned the production and import of opium. In 1813 smoking the drug was made illegal, but smuggled quantities kept increasing. Finally, in 1839 Chinese officials seized 20,000 chests of opium from British merchants in Guangzhou, and the first of two Opium Wars broke out.

Above: The wooden junks of the Chinese forces were no match for the iron steamships of the British in the Opium Wars.

Right: Chinese workers packing crates of porcelain bound for Europe.

Trade with Europe

During the 19th century cotton goods became a major Chinese export, along with traditional silk. Europeans were keen to buy Chinese porcelain, furniture, and lacquer ware, and sales of tea to Britain soared. Goods were paid for in silver, but since China bought few goods in return, European merchants increasingly smuggled in opium from India to earn some of the silver back.

CHINA IN THE 19TH CENTURY

MONGOLIA
MANCHURIA
XINJIANG
Beijing
QINGHAI
KOREA
TIBET
HENAN
JAPAN
GUIZHOU
TAIWAN
Hong Kong

Manchu China

The map shows the border of China in 1800. The Manchu lost territory steadily throughout the 19th century, including Hong Kong (to Britain), Macau (to Portugal), Taiwan and the Pescadores (to Japan), northwestern Xinjiang and Outer Manchuria (to Russia), as well as tributaries such as Indo-China (to France), Burma (to Britain), and Korea and the Ryukyu Islands (to Japan). At the end of the first Opium War, the Treaty of Nanjing forced the opening of five treaty ports to the British. By the terms of the treaty the island of Hong Kong was also handed over, and the mainland peninsula of Kowloon was added in 1860. In 1898 the New Territories were granted to Britain on a 99-year lease.

Right: This satirical drawing shows—from left—Queen Victoria (from Great Britain), Kaiser Wilhelm (from Germany), Tzar Nicholas (from Russia), Marianne (from France), and Emperor Mutsuhito (from Japan), as they are about to cut up China, as though it were a cake to be shared among them.

China Resists European Colonization

Although China never became a colony of any Western power, its economy was dominated by Europeans who created enclaves, such as Shanghai, and treated the Chinese with contempt. This led to frequent nationalist uprisings against foreigners.

Chinese government officials at the end of the 19th century.

The Taiping Rebellion

The Taiping rebellion consisted of a series of uprisings between 1851 and 1864. The rebellion's leader, Hong Xiuquan, was convinced by a dream that he was Jesus Christ's brother and the savior of China. His preaching gained him many followers, who combined Christian beliefs with communist ideals. They captured Nanking in 1853 and introduced many socialist policies, such as the abolition of private property. After Hong's death, the Manchus crushed the rebellion, in which about 20 million people had been killed.

Hong Xiuquan (1814–64) had failed to get a place in the Chinese civil service before he declared himself "Heavenly King of the Great Peace."

Commander Perry Arrives in Japan

In 1853 Commodore Perry steamed into Edo (Tokyo) Bay and presented a treaty of friendship and commerce to the emperor's representatives, implying that he would use power if the Japanese did not comply. He returned in 1854 with an even more powerful fleet of ships and the government signed the Treaty of Kanagawa, which opened up two ports to US trade.

Right: Until Perry arrived the Japanese had never seen a steamship. As this contemporary Japanese illustration shows, many thought it was a devilish machine.

Japan

The military government established at the beginning of the 17th century stayed in power until the mid-19th century. Under this system, political power lay with the shogun at Kyoto, who controlled the local barons. All contact with foreigners was shunned, and despite repeated attempts by Russia and America to trade, Japan maintained its isolationist position. During the 1850s American ships tried to force trading contacts, which led to conflict. Anti-foreign feelings eventually caused a civil war in Japan (1867–68) and the overthrow of the shogun. He was replaced by the emperor. Under the emperor, Japan decided to compete with the West and began a rapid program of industrialization. It also built a powerful army and navy and set out to dominate East Asia. In wars against China and Russia, it gained more territories, including Taiwan (1895) and Korea (1910).

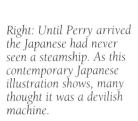

Japanese pistol used during the civil war of 1867–68.

End of the Tokugawa Dynasty

Even before Perry's arrival, many of the great clans resented the Tokugawa government and supported the emperor in Kyoto. After Japanese ports were opened up to trade, the presence of foreign ships enraged these clans even further. Young samurai attacked the ships, but their attacks were quelled by a multinational force in 1863–64. Civil war followed in 1867–68, further weakening the shogunate. Tokugawa Yoshinobu, the last shogun, resigned in 1868, and Emperor Mutsuhito began the Meiji government.

Left: A samurai warrior's suit of armor, from the 1870s. It was during this time that the Japanese government officially abolished the samurai class of professional warriors.

JAPANESE EXPANSION 1895–1910

Japan

Territory acquired by 1910

SAKHALIN
KURIL ISLANDS
JAPAN
KOREA
PORT ARTHUR
EDO
KYOTO
RYUKYU ISLANDS
TAIWAN
PACIFIC OCEAN

Japan Dominates East Asia

Japan transformed itself from an isolated, conservative country to a great economic and military nation in just over 30 years. From acquiring its surrounding islands, it went on to fight modern wars to gain a mainland empire. In 1910 Japan extended its empire by formally annexing Korea, which it renamed Chosen. Japan continued to expand its realm and by the end of World War I gained commercial rights in Mongolia and Manchuria.

Left: Statue of a geisha from the 19th century.

The Meiji Restoration

Prince Mutsuhito's accession to the throne marked the beginning of what is called the Meiji restoration. Influential Japanese and Westerners helped to strengthen the government and unify the country. Meiji abolished the feudal system of shoguns, daimyos, and samurais. New political, economic, and social systems were established and Western-style systems of law, administration, and taxation were introduced.

KEY EVENTS

1853
Commodore Matthew Perry arrives in Japan.

1854
Perry forces Japan to begin trading with the United States.

1863–64
Western naval force bombards Kagoshima and Shimonoseki in response to attacks on Western shipping.

1867–68
Civil war after Choshu and Satsuma clans oppose shogun.

1868
Emperor Meiji takes power from the last shogun; the capital is moved from Kyoto to Edo (modern Tokyo); the feudal system is abolished.

1879
Japan takes over the Ryukyu Islands.

1889
Western-style constitution and parliament are introduced.

1894–95
Japan defeats China in the Sino-Japanese War.

1904–05
Japan defeats Russia in the Russo-Japanese War

1910
Japan annexes Korea.

Japan Industrializes

Japan was one of the few Asian countries not colonized by the West. This was mainly due to industrialization, which began in 1873 when the Meiji government formally abolished the old feudal system. The Japanese government invited Western industrialists and engineers to advise Japan on how to modernize. Japanese businessmen set up coal mines, steel mills, shipyards, and factories.

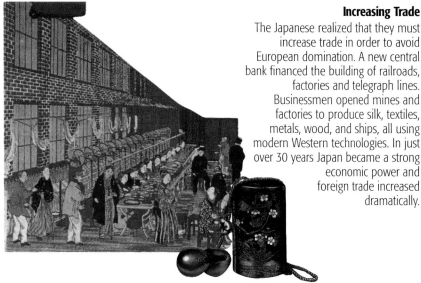

Increasing Trade

The Japanese realized that they must increase trade in order to avoid European domination. A new central bank financed the building of railroads, factories and telegraph lines. Businessmen opened mines and factories to produce silk, textiles, metals, wood, and ships, all using modern Western technologies. In just over 30 years Japan became a strong economic power and foreign trade increased dramatically.

Well-equipped and organized Japanese troops fend off the Chinese during the Sino-Japanese War of 1894–95.

A Japanese cartoon showing a Japanese emperor baiting a Russian bear.

Army Reforms

Japan reorganized and modernized its military in order to compete with Western powers. In 1872 the emperor decreed a universal military service. The Japanese government brought in French officers to remodel the army and British seamen to help create a new navy equipped with modern ships. With its stronger military, Japan was able to look for new territories to colonize.

Sino-Japanese War

In 1894 a growing economic crisis in Korea prompted the Tonghak revolt. China and Japan intervened, but then began a struggle themselves for domination of the area. The Japanese navy crushed the Chinese at the Battle of the Yellow Sea, while the army defeated the Chinese in Manchuria. Under the Treaty of Shimonoseki, Japan gained Taiwan and the Pescadores, while Korea became briefly independent. Japan was also awarded the Liaodong Peninsula in southern Manchuria, but Russia, France, and Germany forced Japan to accept a payment instead.

Relations with Russia

In 1898 Japan and Russia signed a treaty pledging Korean independence. In 1900, however, Russian armies began to enter northern Korea. They attacked the Russian-controlled Port Arthur in southern Manchuria, starting the Russo-Japanese War. The Japanese defeated the Russians in less than 18 months. In the treaty of 1905, Japan was awarded the Liaodong Peninsula and the southern half of Sakhalin. Russia was also forced to recognize the predominant interests of Japan in Korea.

1804
Haiti becomes first country in Latin America to gain independence.

1810–11
Unsuccessful revolt in Mexico.

1821
Mexico independent.

1838
United Provinces of Central America splits into Guatemala, El Salvador, Honduras, Nicaragua and Costa Rica.

1844
Santo Domingo independent.

1862
Honduras becomes a British colony; Jamaica independent.

1884
Costa Rica grants land to Minor C. Keith, founder of the United Fruit Company.

1899
Cuba independent.

1903
Panama gains independence from Colombia.

Unity in Central America

The United Provinces of Central America, formed in 1823, consisted of Guatemala, El Salvador, Honduras, Nicaragua, and Costa Rica. It dissolved in civil war between 1838 and 1840. Various attempts were made to reunite it, but none succeeded for any length of time. Guatemalan President Justo Rufino Barrios tried in the 1880s and was killed in the process. A union of Honduras, Nicaragua, and El Salvador as the Greater Republic of Central America lasted from 1896–98.

Central America and the Caribbean

The Spanish and Portuguese colonial powers were ousted from all of Latin America in a remarkably short period of time, from 1818 to 1828, leaving only some colonies in the Caribbean. Independence was gained through a combination of local rebellions and events in Europe. Mexico began its revolt in 1810, led by the Catholic priest Miguel Hidalgo y Costilla. The initial revolt failed, and Mexico did not gain its independence until 1821. Central Americans won freedom in the same year, with Costa Rica, El Salvador, Guatemala, Honduras, and Nicaragua becoming part of Mexico in 1822. The following year they broke away again and formed the United Provinces of Central America. By 1847 each of the five states was an independent republic. Panama was a Colombian province until 1903, when it rebelled with the help of the United States and became independent. British Honduras (present-day Belize) became a British colony in 1862 and only gained independence in 1981.

Economy

In 1884 the President of Costa Rica, Oreamuno, gave the American businessman Minor C. Keith huge tracts of land in exchange for building railroads. Keith grew bananas there and throughout Central America and the Caribbean. His company, United Fruit, became the largest employer in Central America and built one of the largest merchant navies in the world. However, the profits from United Fruit and other US companies did not go to ordinary people; they were paid to corrupt local politicians or exported north with the produce.

Justo Rufino Barrios, president of Guatemala (1873–1885), was known for his liberal reforms and attempts to reunify Central America.

A locally made vase shows the three constituents of the Latin American population: indigenous, Spanish, and African.

A Creole overseer on a banana plantation in Central America. Once slavery was abolished, the backbreaking work was carried out by local inhabitants, including freed slaves.

CENTRAL AMERICA AND THE CARIBBEAN

UNITED STATES OF AMERICA

ATLANTIC OCEAN

MEXICO
1821

MEXICAN GULF

BAHAMAS
1973

DOMINICAN REPUBLIC
(INDI. FROM HAITI)
1844

CUBA
(INDIP. DA SPAGNA)
1902

HAITI
1804

GIAMAICA
1862

PUERTO RICO
(FROM SPAIN TO U.S.A.)
1898

UNITED PROVINCES
OF CENTRAL
AMERICA
1823

CARIBBEAN
SEA

PANAMA
(IND. FROM COLOMBIA)
1903

GREAT COLOMBIA

Fighting for Freedom

Spanish and Portuguese colonies in Central America and the Caribbean gained their independence during the 19th century. The map shows the dates when countries became independent. Haiti was the first country to free itself from foreign rule in 1804 as the result of a slave revolt against plantation owners that began in 1791. The revolt was led by a slave named François Toussant L'Ouverture. Despite help from the British and French, independence was finally proclaimed on January 1, 1804.

South America

Spain and Portugal were greatly weakened by events in Europe, especially Napoleon's invasion of the Iberian Peninsula in 1807. Simón Bolívar and other American liberators quickly took the opportunity to rise up against and defeat the Europeans. But the newly liberated Latin Americans did not find it easy to make their new republics work efficiently and peacefully, and ambitious military leaders or wealthy landowners often seized power. Although slaves were freed by the end of the 19th century, independence did not bring much economic benefit to most ordinary people.

Peru

Peru declared its independence in 1821. The Spanish were defeated by General Sucre's troops three years later. Caudillos, or "military leaders," fought for control of the new nation, and stability was only achieved when General Ramón Castilla became president in 1845.

Right: Peruvian patriot José Olaya.

Chile

The Chileans began their revolt in 1810, when a provisional republic was declared. General Bernardo O'Higgins led the fight for independence. In 1814 he joined forces with the army of the Argentinian liberator, José de San Martin. The two men led the "Army of the Andes" from Argentina over the Andes into Chile, and in 1817 defeated the Spanish. Chile gained independence in 1818, and O'Higgins served as "supreme director" until 1823. He made sweeping reforms, but was forced to resign after revolts in the provinces.

Chileans rejoice beneath their new flag.

Brazil

Brazil declared independence in 1822, and Pedro I (1798–1834), son of John VI of Portugal, became emperor. He was forced to resign in 1831 and left his throne to his five-year-old son, Pedro II (1826–91), who ruled from 1840 for more than 50 years. Despite wars against Argentina and Paraguay, Brazil prospered; agriculture and industry expanded, railroads were built, and between 1870 and 1888 slavery was abolished. Brazil became a republic in 1889.

LATIN AMERICA

PANAMA 1903 · CARIBBEAN SEA · GUYANA IND. FROM BRITAIN 1966 · VENEZUELA 1821 · NUOVA GRANADA 1831 · SURINAME IND. FROM HOLLAND 1975 · GREAT COLOMBIA · ECUADOR 1830 · FRENCH GUYANA · BRAZILIAN EMPIRE · PERU 1824 · BOLIVIA 1825 · PARAGUAY 1811 · CHILE 1818 · UNITED PROVINCES OF RIO DELLA PLATA (ARGENTINA) 1816 · PACIFIC OCEAN · URUGUAY 1828 · ATLANTIC OCEAN

Latin America with Dates of Independence
The map shows the countries of Latin America with the date by which independence was gained. The largest country in South America, Brazil, won its freedom from Portugal without bloodshed. The Portuguese court had moved to Brazil during the Napoleonic Wars, and in 1815 the colony was made a kingdom. In 1822 independence was declared by Pedro I (1798–1834), who became emperor.

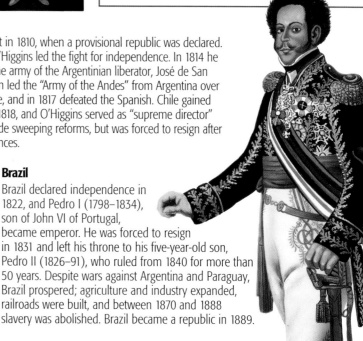

Simón Bolívar

Bolívar was South America's greatest general. Known as "the Liberator," he gained independence for Bolivia, Colombia, Ecuador, Peru, and Venezuela. Bolívar became president of Gran Colombia in 1819, and the area formerly known as Upper Peru took the name Bolivia in his honor. Rather than creating many independent nations, Bolívar had hoped to form a united Andean republic. But his dream was never realized and he became disillusioned by the political disagreements that put paid to unity.

Below: This detail from a fresco in the Simon Bolivar Amphitheatre in Mexico, shows the American creole soldier and statesman fighting Spanish royalist troops.

Below: Antonio José de Sucre (1795–1830) was born in Venezuela. He was the most able of Simón Bolívar's generals and helped to liberate Ecuador, Peru, and Bolivia. He served as president of Bolivia. The nation's legal capital, Sucre, is named after him.

Von Humboldt

In 1799 the German scientist Alexander von Humboldt (1769–1859, right) set out for Central and South America. He spent five years studying the geology and biology of Latin America, collecting a vast number of samples. On his return to Europe in 1804 he met Simón Bolívar, and it is said that he told Bolívar that South America was ripe for revolution.

Ending Slavery

Ideas about slavery changed markedly between the 18th and 19th centuries. In 1750 almost no one seriously questioned the existence of slavery, but by 1888 it had been abolished from the Americas and Europe. The ideas of Enlightenment thinkers such as Locke and Montesquieu led people to reflect carefully about equality and some began to think that slavery was unacceptable. In America, a radical Protestant group called the Quakers were among the first to mount organized opposition to slavery and by 1787 it had been eliminated from the northern states.

Great Britain

The international antislavery movement was largely organized by the British. During the 1780s antislavery reformers had decided to work first to end the trading of slaves (rather then the abolition of slavery itself which they felt would come naturally once the sale of slaves had been abolished). By 1807 the British parliament had voted to eliminate the slave trade throughout the British Empire. They also sent ships to the coast of Africa to arrest any slaving ships. By 1865 an estimated 150,000 slaves had been emancipated in this way. These people were often sent to Sierra Leone or Liberia, two African states founded by Britain and the United States, respectively, as homes for freed slaves.

Left: William Wilberforce was the founder of the Society for the Abolition of the Slave Trade. A British politician, he introduced a bill into parliament each year calling for the end of the slave trade; he was finally successful in 1808.

Below: A procession in Wiltshire, England, on February 3, 1808, after the slave trade was outlawed in the British Empire.

Above: Slaves were transported from Africa to the Americas in dreadful conditions and many died during the long journey.

Resurgence of Slavery

Despite the advances made in ending slavery there were some setbacks in the early years of the 19th century. World demand for products such as cotton, coffee, and sugar, led plantation owners in the southern United States, Brazil, and Cuba to actually increase their demand for slaves and many more Africans were transported across the Atlantic. Slavery did not end in the US until after the Civil War and it continued in Cuba until 1886 and in Brazil until 1888.

Right: Slaves harvesting coffee in Brazil. Between 1800 and 1855 about two million Africans were brought to Brazil.

Slave Revolts

Slaves also often tried to take the matter into their own hands by organizing revolts against their owners. A revolt in Haiti was successful in ending slavery and in freeing the colony from its Spanish overlords. Other revolts in the Caribbean during the 1820s and 1830s were brutally repressed.

Abolition of Slavery

Slavery was gradually abolished in Latin America as the various countries achieved independence. In the 1820s, British antislavery reformers abandoned the goal of gradually emancipating slaves and began to demand a complete and immediate end to slavery. They were successful in 1833 when their parliament abolished the right of British subjects to hold slaves. The other European colonial powers gradually followed suit, until slavery no longer existed.

1843
Argentina abolishes slavery.

1845
36 British Navy ships are assigned to the Anti-Slavery Squadron, making it one of the largest fleets in the world.

1847
Sweden abolishes slavery.

1848
Denmark abolishes slavery.

1851
Brazil ends slave trade.

1854
Peru abolishes slavery.

1854
Venezuela abolishes slavery.

1862
Cuba abolishes slave trade.

1863
Slavery abolished in Dutch colonies.

1865
United States abolishes slavery.

1873
Puerto Rico abolishes slavery.

1886
Cuba abolishes slavery.

1888
Brazil abolishes slavery.

1890
Brussels Act: Treaty granting anti-slavery powers the right to stop and search ships for slaves.

1896
France abolishes slavery in Madagascar.

1897
Zanzibar abolishes slavery.

World Trade

During the 19th century world trade was dominated by the industrialized nations of Europe and the United States. They traded manufactured goods and food among themselves and, increasingly, with countries in Asia, Latin America, and Africa. The infrastructure, such as railroads, roads and ports, that was required to support global trade was built by the industrialized nations in many parts of the world. However, economies in traditional societies were often destroyed by the demands of the Europeans and any opposition to them was usually brutally repressed. Large gold rushes in California, Australia, South Africa, and Canada increased the supply of money available and helped sustain international trade.

Gold standard

Increasing global trade required an international standard for currencies. Britain adopted the gold standard in 1821, by which different country's currencies were convertible into gold at a fixed rate and international debts were met in gold. If a country had a trade deficit, there would be an outflow of gold, reducing its money supply. This would lead to lower prices, which would encourage exports.

1 *Local people in the Niger Delta extract oil from palms using traditional methods.*

2 *British merchants collect the palm oil and ship it back to Britain.*

Global Trading

Industrialized countries in Europe imported raw materials from their colonies, turned them into manufactured goods in their factories, and then either sold them at home or re-exported them back to the colonies. The series of illustrations above shows how the British imported palm oil from the Niger Delta, in Africa, and used it to manufacture soap, which was then exported all over the world.

WORLD SHIPPING ROUTES AND COALING STATIONS

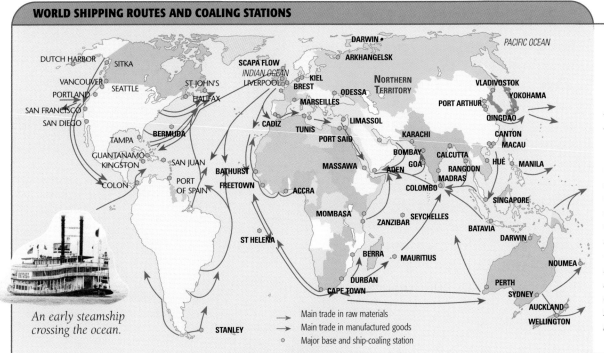

An early steamship crossing the ocean.

→ Main trade in raw materials
→ Main trade in manufactured goods
○ Major base and ship-coaling station

Increased Trade
The canals opened at Suez (1869) and Panama (1914) cut voyage times around Africa and South America, and between 1850 and 1914 the world's merchant fleet expanded almost fourfold. Fast and efficient sea routes, combined with the opening up of fertile lands in Canada, the United States, Australia, Russia, and Argentina, brought down the price of wheat and other staple foods in industrialized nations.

3 *The palm oil is manufactured into soap in British factories ready for consumption at home or re-export.*

4 *Families in Africa, where the raw material originated, buy imported British soap. Soap was marketed as a "civilizing" product.*

Ship Design
The introduction of steam had a great impact on trade. The first Mississippi steamboat left New Orleans in 1812, and seven years later the American-built Savannah became the first steamship to cross the Atlantic. By 1835 paddle-steamers were making regular transatlantic crossings. Ports were modernized and enlarged to handle the new, bigger ships and larger cargoes. Clippers were still the fastest ships, however, speeding to Europe with wool from Australia and tea from China.

Art and Cultural Exchange

The establishment of European colonial empires was often a painful—and sometimes a disastrous—experience for both the local inhabitants and the colonizers. Clashes of cultural mores and religious beliefs were common and frequently violent, while the Europeans' desire to enrich themselves in the colonies led to the economic exploitation of indigenous peoples. Notwithstanding this, there were some interesting and positive results, especially in the arts and social sciences. Contact between Western societies and other cultures opened up new ways of seeing the world, and artists on all sides were influenced by each other.

Detail of a fresco from the Ajanta Caves in India, showing a princess and her servant. The Buddhist paintings and sculptures in the caves date to the 2nd century CE, but they were lost to our knowledge until some British soldiers rediscovered them in 1819. Archeologists and art historians have studied the caves closely.

Left: With their exotic coloring and style, Japanese prints like this one captivated the French art world of the 1870s. Critics and artists both sought to celebrate Japanese art.

Exotic Influences

The Impressionist artist Claude Monet admired Japanese art and its influence had already surfaced in his work. Then, in the 1870s, Japanese prints became enormously popular in Paris and the artist saw a way of combining his love of oriental art with the chance of making some lucrative sales. This portrait of his wife in Japanese costume, entitled *La Japonaise*, was included in the Impressionist exhibition of 1876.

Archeology

Archeology is the systematic study of the past through its physical remains. People have always been curious about the past, but archeology as a discipline of the social sciences only really began in the 19th century. Professional and amateur archeologists began to develop theories about history and also to excavate old cities and areas and then carefully examine their findings. The Institute for Archeological Correspondence was founded in Rome in 1829, so that they could exchange information and opinions.

This intricately carved ivory statue from Benin, in Africa, shows slave traders of Portuguese origin.

Indigenous Artists

Non-Western artists in the colonies began to make paintings and sculptures of the new arrivals from Europe. Initially, their art was executed in their own styles and using traditional techniques. Then gradually, as they saw more Western art, they too were influenced by what they saw and their was a mingling of styles. With music, the European style often completely prevailed over the indigenous one, which disappeared before people had a chance to record it.

Right: A carved wooden mask of a Maori mythological figure from New Zealand.

Paul Gauguin

The French artist Paul Gauguin (1848–1903) was a leading Postimpressionist painter. In 1891, frustrated by lack of recognition at home and financially destitute, he sailed to the Pacific islands to escape European civilization and "everything that is artificial and conventional." He lived there for the rest of his life and all his paintings from that time on were strongly influence by his "tropical paradise."

Right: This painting is called Nafea Faaipoipo *(When are you Getting Married?). Gauguin painted it in 1892.*

Collecting Indigenous Art

Missionaries, explorers, and colonial officials often collected works of art by indigenous peoples. They brought them home with them and either studied them themselves or passed them along to ethnologists. These artifacts began to be displayed in museums at this time.

Gold Fever

Gold has been known and highly valued since ancient times, but in 1821 when Great Britain introduced the gold standard (see page 26), it became a truly global currency. As new territories opened up in Canada, Australia, New Zealand, South Africa, and many other places too, gold was often discovered and a great "gold rush" would follow. The many gold rushes of the 19th century contributed to the political and economic growth of the surrounding regions, helping to develop and enlarge new colonies. The discovery of gold usually led to the construction of railroads and telegraph lines as well as cities with banks, roads, businesses, and bustling social activities.

Right: Prospectors arriving in the Klondike region. Many of the miners, who were mainly men (although there were some women too), carried everything they owned on their backs.

The Klondike

The discovery of gold along the Klondike River, near Dawson, in Yukon, Canada, in 1896 led to the last great gold rush of the 19th century. News of the strike spread fast and thousands of prospectors had arrived by 1898. The population of the once tiny town of Klondike swelled to more than 40,000, almost causing a famine since there was barely enough food to go around. People from all walks of life headed for the Yukon from as far away as New York, Britain, and Australia. Surprisingly, a large proportion were professionals, such as teachers and doctors, who gave up respectable careers to make the journey. Most of them knew that their chances of finding significant amounts of gold were slim, but they went anyway, just for the adventure. As with other gold rushes, the arrival of many adventurous souls in search of fortune contributed greatly to the economic development of the entire region.

Below: There were several gold rushes in Australia. The scene below shows the early stages of the gold rush in Victoria in 1851. This was the biggest of the Australian rushes and contributed greatly to the political and economic development of Victoria and the city of Melbourne.

Above: Chinese gold miners during the gold rush in California. The Chinese had a good knowledge of minefields and the best technology to extract gold efficiently. Chinese workers migrated to many of the gold rush areas. Many stayed on, creating the beginnings of a multicultural society in some parts of the New World.

GOLD RUSHES

1829
Georgia Gold Rush, in the Appalachians, USA.

1848–52
California Gold Rush, in the Sierra Nevada, USA.

1851
Victoria Gold Rush, in Australia.

1851
Queen Charlotte's Gold Rush, is the first of several gold rushes in British Columbia, Canada.

1861–63
Central Otago Gold Rush, in New Zealand.

1880s onward
Tierra del Fuego, in Argentina.

1886
Witwatersrand Gold Rush, in South Africa, leads to the founding of Johannesburg.

1893
Kalgoorlie Gold Rush, in Western Australia.

1898–99
Klondike Gold Rush, in the Yukon, Canada.

Australia

The British explorer James Cook claimed New South Wales in Australia for Britain. The arrival of the British in Sydney Cove resulted in catastrophic changes for the Aboriginal people who had been living in Australia for at least 40,000 years. The British claimed New South Wales was unoccupied, largely based on Cook's incorrect reports that the Aboriginals were not settled there. New South Wales was established by the British as a penal settlement. Western Australia and Queensland were also founded as penal colonies, but free settlers colonized South Australia and Victoria. Convicts built roads, churches, and government buildings until as late as 1868, even as growing numbers of immigrants arrived from 1830 onward. They were attracted by the opening up of grazing land for merino sheep and beef cattle, and later by the gold rush.

Exploration

By 1804, Matthew Flinders in his sloop "Investigator" had circumnavigated Australia and proved it was an island continent. In 1813, explorers crossed the Blue Mountains west of Sydney and found land suitable for crops and cattle. Between 1820 and 1850, inland explorers discovered more pastoral land in eastern Australia as well as large rivers such as the Murray and the Darling. Others discovered hot, arid regions, unsuitable for farming. Burke and Wills (above), with their camels and horses, first crossed the continent in 1860–61.

Above: A view of Sydney from the North Shore.

Below: An entire British family arrives in Adelaide. Australia was an expensive, six-week-long sea voyage from Europe. Immigrants leaving Britain knew that they would not see home again.

AUSTRALIA

1770
James Cook lands at Botany Bay.

1778
First British convicts arrive on the First Fleet.

1801–03
Flinders circumnavigates Australia.

1813
Blue Mountains crossed.

1817
Governor Lachlan Macquarie formally adopts the name "Australia" for the Colony.

1825
Tasmania secedes from New South Wales.

1829–36
Free colonies established in Australia.

1851
Gold rush in New South Wales and Victoria.

1901
British colonial rule of Australia ends.

Aborigines

The Australian colony's first Governor, Arthur Phillip, treated the Aborigines with respect, but most of his successors did not. There was much violent conflict. In their search for farming country, the Europeans invaded Aboriginal food-gathering and hunting territories, and forcibly occupied their lands. The Aborigines had no choice but to give up their traditional way of life. Infectious European diseases such as influenza and measles, as well as extreme poverty, caused the deaths of many Aborigines.

LAND USE IN AUSTRALIA

INDIAN OCEAN

PACIFIC OCEAN

• DARWIN

NORTHERN TERRITORY

A U S T R A L I A

WESTERN AUSTRALIA

QUEENSLAND

SOUTH AUSTRALIA

BRISBANE •

• PERTH

SOUTHERN OCEAN

• ADELAIDE

NEW SOUTH WALES

CANBERRA •
VICTORIA
• SYDNEY

• MELBOURNE

TASMANIA

By 1845   By 1900

By 1860   Since 1900

By 1880   Not used

The Search for "Fresh Pastures"

When Charles Darwin visited New South Wales in 1836, he observed that the settlers were obsessed with money and sheep. Darwin also noted the continual push for "fresh pastures." Successive colonial governors failed to control the grab for land. However, by 1850 these so-called "squatters" had seized millions of acres of land. For most of the 19th century, the Australian colonies existed separately. Gradually, however, the colonials came to see themselves as Australians rather than as Victorians or Queenslanders. As no single colony could produce a defense force, protecting the coastline required a national strategy. In 1898 a new constitution was agreed, with the British monarch retained as head of state. British colonial rule ended in 1901 when Edmund Barton became prime minister of the Commonwealth of Australia with its new capital in Canberra.

New Zealand

WAITANGI •

□ Territory purchased from
Ngai Tahu 1844–64   AUCKLAND •

□ Center of Maori King
Movement 1858

□ Maori land confiscated   NORTH ISLAND
by Government 1864–67

TASMAN SEA

• WELLINGTON

• CHRISTCHURCH

SOUTH ISLAND
PACIFIC
OCEAN

• DUNEDIN

☆ STEWART ISLAND

The New Zealand Wars, also known as the Land Wars, were fought between 1845 and 1872 mainly over land ownership issues. The Treaty of Waitangi was supposed to guarantee Maori ownership of land and fishing rights, but large tracts of land were confiscated by the government in 1863.

The first Europeans to reach New Zealand were the Dutch explorer Abel Tasman and his crew in 1642. No Europeans returned until British explorer James Cook's voyage of 1768–71. Cook reached New Zealand in 1769 and mapped almost the entire coastline. After that, New Zealand was visited by whaling, sealing, and trading ships from Europe and North America. They traded food and goods, especially metal tools and weapons, with the Maori in exchange for timber, food, artifacts and water. From the early 19th century, Christian missionaries began to settle in New Zealand, eventually converting most of the Maori population.

Above: Settlers introduced sheep which flourished on the good agricultural land.

Below: Maori warriors prepare for war by dancing the Haka.

Settlers and the Maori

At first, most Maori welcomed the new arrivals, trading their decorative wooden carvings, food, flax mats, and shrunken human heads for metal products such as nails, axes, and guns, as well as rum. In the 1820s some Maori chiefs, including Hongi Hika, traded goods for muskets, with which they attacked and killed their tribal enemies. Musket use spread south, in a series of tribal wars that disrupted the traditional Maori way of life.

Treaty Of Waitangi

In 1840, the Treaty of Waitangi appointed Queen Victoria as the supreme ruler, or sovereign, of New Zealand. In return, Maori chiefs were promised protection and possession of their property and fishing grounds if they agreed to sell land only to the Crown. However, such transactions created problems, as Maori land was held communally rather than individually owned, and some chiefs refused to sign the Treaty. Under the Treaty, the Maori people became British subjects.

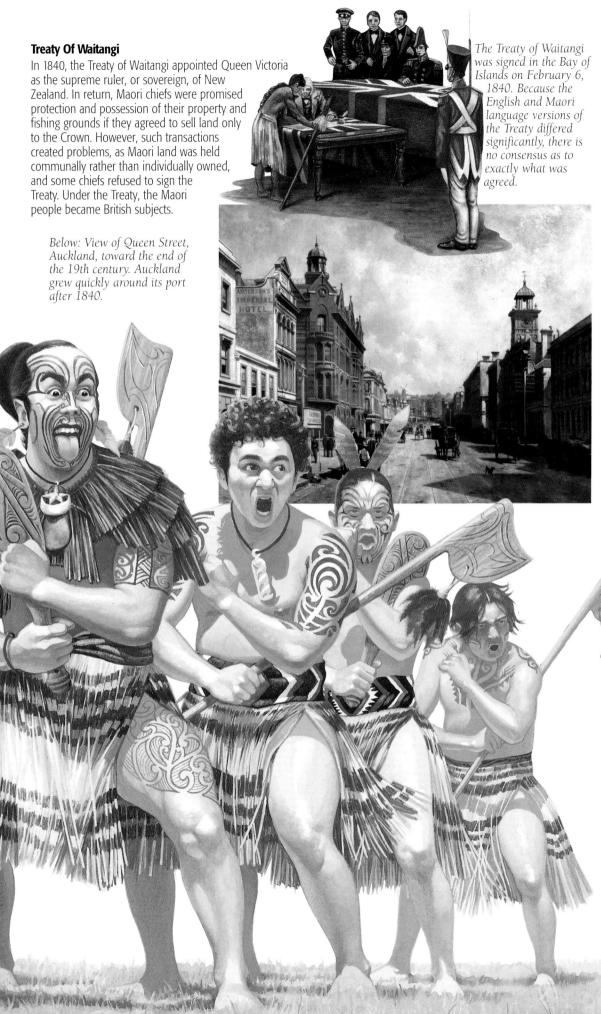

The Treaty of Waitangi was signed in the Bay of Islands on February 6, 1840. Because the English and Maori language versions of the Treaty differed significantly, there is no consensus as to exactly what was agreed.

Below: View of Queen Street, Auckland, toward the end of the 19th century. Auckland grew quickly around its port after 1840.

A Farming Economy

More and more settlers came after 1840, mainly from Great Britain and Ireland. By 1859 they outnumbered the original Maori inhabitants, many of whom died of European diseases to which they had no resistance. Farming became the economic backbone of the country with meat, wool, and dairy products exported mainly to Great Britain.

The Pacific

European exploration of Oceania began in 1520 when three Spanish ships commanded by Magellan stopped off at the Mariana Islands on their way to the Philippines. In the 17th to 19th centuries rivalry between European colonial powers, opportunities for trade, and Christian missions, drove further European exploration and eventual settlement. Some of the first white settlers were convicts who had escaped from Australian penal colonies. Missionaries reached some islands to find white people already living there.

This 19th century illustration shows French explorer Monsieur de Lapérouse (1741–88), being welcomed by the inhabitants of the island of Maui, Sandwich Islands, Hawaii, May 28, 1789. Lapérouse continued onto Australia from where he posted his diaries back to Paris. This was lucky, because after he and his crew set sail from Australia they were never seen again.

Right: This colored engraving shows indigenous inhabitants of the Marquesas Islands, from Histoire des Voyages Autour du Monde by J. Dufay, 1826.

Other Colonies in the Pacific

The United States officially annexed Hawaii in 1898. A year later the US made American Samoa a colony. Germany claimed several territories in the Pacific, including part of New Guinea (1884), the German Marshal Islands (1885), the German Mariana Islands (1899), the German Caroline Islands (1899), and German Samoa.

The French in the Pacific

French colonies in Oceania included New Caledonia, the various island groups which make up French Polynesia (including the Society Islands, the Marquesas, the Tuamotus), and–jointly with Britain–the New Hebrides. French Catholic missionaries arrived in Tahiti in 1834 although they were sent away two years later. In 1842, Tahiti and Tahuata were declared French protectorates, so that Catholic missionaries could work undisturbed. In 1880, France annexed Tahiti, changing its status from a protectorate to a colony. In the 1880s, France claimed the Tuamotu Archipelago.

Below: Like Britain, France sent criminals to penal colonies. New Caledonia in the Pacific received dissidents like the Communards, as well as convicted criminals.

Pacific Boundaries

The Pacific Ocean covers almost one-third of the surface of the planet and is made up of about 25,000 islands. It is traditionally divided into three areas on the basis of the peoples that live there: Melanesia, Micronesia, and Polynesia.

Below: Drawings of dancing costumes worn in Fiji in the 19th century.

Above: Map showing Australia, New Zealand, and the Pacific Islands made by a German cartographer in about 1850.

Missionaries

Protestants in Britain were shocked by tales of human sacrifice, cannibalism, and the killing of babies that filtered back with early explorers of Oceania. In 1797 the London Missionary Society landed missionaries in Tahiti, the Marquesas Islands, and Tonga to put a stop to all this. In time, Christian missionaries did convert most of the population, destroying unique religious cultures and works of art that they believed were heathen.

Above: A Hawaiian sculpture of Ku, god of the earth and of war.

The British in the Pacific

The British government sent explorer James Cook to the Pacific in 1768 to observe the transit of Venus and to go south in search of the Great South Land. Cook made three long voyages in Oceania and was eventually killed in Hawaii. The British subsequently laid claim to a string of islands across the Pacific: Fiji (1874), the Cook Islands (1880), the New Hebrides (1887, but governed jointly with France), the Phoenix Islands (1889), the Gilbert and Ellis Islands (1892), and the Solomans.

Africa Before Colonization

During the first part of the 19th century most of Africa, then known to Europeans as the "Dark Continent," was free from outside imperialist powers. During the course of the century explorers, adventurers, and Christian missionaries journeyed widely through the continent, including the northern deserts and central rainforests. The Europeans became aware that there were vast, untapped resources in Africa, including diamonds and gold.

Early colonization

Before 1880 only two African regions were colonized by Europeans on a large scale. Northern Algeria was invaded by the French in 1830, and in southern Africa the original Dutch Cape Colony had been seized by the British. Then came the formation of the Afrikaner states of Transvaal and Orange Free State. Apart from this, there were Portuguese territories in Angola and on the east coast, as well as Spanish, British, and French trading stations and those slaving ports that still existed.

African Empires

African leaders continued to build their empires after the arrival of Europeans. As European countries developed more of a demand for Africa's resources, including slaves, they began to claim more power in the continent. Despite this, during the 18th century and early part of the 19th century the majority of African leaders managed to retain political control of their kingdoms.

Exploration

The best-known African explorers were David Livingstone and Henry Morton Stanley (1841–1904), a British-American journalist. Livingstone first crossed the continent in the 1850s. In 1871 an American newspaper hired Stanley to look for Livingstone, of whom nothing had been heard for some time. When he met Livingstone on the shores of Lake Tanganyika, Stanley greeted him with the famous words: "Dr Livingstone, I presume?"

Below: Scottish missionary and explorer David Livingstone traveled through Africa in 1850 with his wife and four small children.

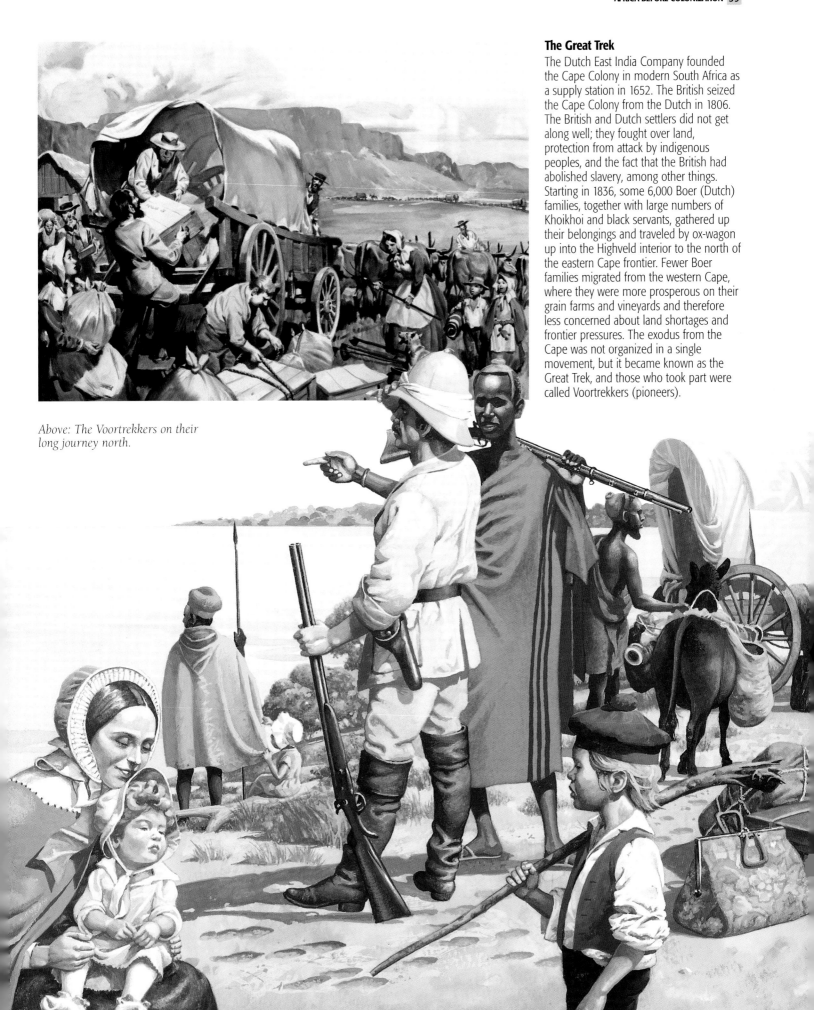

*Above: The Voortrekkers on their
long journey north.*

The Great Trek

The Dutch East India Company founded the Cape Colony in modern South Africa as a supply station in 1652. The British seized the Cape Colony from the Dutch in 1806. The British and Dutch settlers did not get along well; they fought over land, protection from attack by indigenous peoples, and the fact that the British had abolished slavery, among other things. Starting in 1836, some 6,000 Boer (Dutch) families, together with large numbers of Khoikhoi and black servants, gathered up their belongings and traveled by ox-wagon up into the Highveld interior to the north of the eastern Cape frontier. Fewer Boer families migrated from the western Cape, where they were more prosperous on their grain farms and vineyards and therefore less concerned about land shortages and frontier pressures. The exodus from the Cape was not organized in a single movement, but it became known as the Great Trek, and those who took part were called Voortrekkers (pioneers).

The Partition of Africa

In the 1860s Europeans became aware that there were large, untapped resources in Africa, including diamonds and gold. During the last quarter of the century they sent armed expeditions to claim exclusive rights over vast territories. Many African peoples resisted, but the Europeans used their advantage of superior weapons to dominate and divide up the continent. By the end of the century most of Africa was under European control.

Mineral Wealth

Two discoveries changed the European attitude to southern Africa: in 1866 diamonds were discovered on the banks of the Orange River, and in 1886 prospectors struck gold near Pretoria. Fortune hunters descended on the region, including Englishman Cecil Rhodes, who gained control of the diamond mines and became prime minister of Cape Colony.

Left: French diplomat Paul Cambon and British prime minister Lord Salisbury discussing Africa in 1899.

Below: This illustration celebrates the Ethiopian victory over the Italians at the battle of Adwa in 1896.

Above: South Africa had some of the richest diamond-bearing territories on the planet. It all began in 1866 on a farm near Hopetown, when a young shepherd named Erasmus Jacobs found a small white pebble on the bank of the Orange River. It was passed on to a neighboring farmer who sent it to Grahamstown to be identified. The pebble turned out to be a 21.25 carat diamond, which came to be known as the "Eureka."

The Berlin Conference

In 1884–85 representatives of 15 European nations met in Berlin to discuss how they would proceed in Africa. The Conference did not give specific territories to specific countries, but it did establish guidelines as to how the Europeans could take over certain areas. This led to rapid, piecemeal, and violent colonization of the entire African continent. Some countries worked through trading ventures such as the German South West and East Africa Companies or the British South Africa Company.

Resistance

Some African states collaborated with the invaders, but most opposed them fiercely. The Mahdist revolt in Sudan and defiance by the Asante proved difficult for the Europeans to quell, but other uprisings were quickly put down. Ethiopia was the only state that successfully opposed an invading colonial army, in this case from Italy. The Italians were definitively beaten at the battle of Adwa in 1896 and forced to withdraw. This defeat of a colonial power and the ensuing recognition of African sovereignty became rallying points for later African nationalists.

AFRICA IN 1913

French
British
German
Portuguese
Belgian
Spanish
Italian
Anglo-Egyptian

MOROCCO
RIO DE ORO
ALGERIA
LIBYA
EGYPT
FRENCH WEST AFRICA
FRENCH EQUATORIAL AFRICA
SUDAN
ERITREA
GOLD COAST
NIGERIA
ETHIOPIA
CAMEROON
UGANDA
ITALIAN SOMALILAND
GABON
KENYA
BELGIAN CONGO
GERMAN EAST AFRICA
ANGOLA
NORTHERN RHODESIA
MOZAMBIQUE
MADAGASCAR
GERMAN SOUTH WEST AFRICA
SOUTHERN RHODESIA
UNION OF SOUTH AFRICA

Slicing it Up

France and Britain were the major players in Africa. The French occupied most of north western Africa, Gabon, and the island of Madagascar in the south. The British controlled most of southern Africa, Kenya, Uganda, Egypt, Nigeria, and other territories. Germany had South West Africa, East Africa, and the Cameroon, while the Italians took Libya, Eritrea, and part of Somaliland. Belgium ruled the Congo and the Portuguese had Angola and Mozambique. Only Ethiopia and Liberia stayed free.

Taken by Force

The imperial powers usually had well organized armies and modern technology to take their colonies by force. With their modern weapons, European armies were able defeat armies that far outnumbered them. The invention of the machine gun in 1884, for example, enabled 320 French troops to overpower 12,000 African soldiers in Chad during a battle in 1899.

KEY DATES

1866
Diamonds found on the Orange River, in South Africa.

1883
French begin conquest of Madagascar.

1884–85
The Berlin Conference.

1885
King Leopold of Belgium establishes Congo Free State.

1886
Gold discovered near Pretoria, in South Africa.

1885
British save Khartoum from Mahdist siege.

1889
Italy establishes first colony in Eritrea.

1890
First Nama rebellion against Germans in South West Africa.

1892
France defeats the Tukulor empire in modern Mali.

1893
France defeat Fon warriors in Dahomey.

1894
Britain occupies Uganda.

1896
Ethiopian victory over Italians at Battle of Adwa.

1898
Kitchener defeats Mahdists at Omdurman.

1900
Britain finally defeats the Asante in West Africa.

NORTHERN AFRICA

1869
Suez Canal opens.

1882
Egypt becomes a protectorate of Britain.

1885
Mahdist forces overrun Khartoum, killing British General Gordon.

1897
German foreign minister Bernard von Bülow describes German colonization of Africa as the search for "a place in the sun."

1898
Fashoda incident on the White Nile in Sudan brings France and Britain to the brink of war; Kirchener finally defeats Mahdists at Omdurman.

1890
Britain gives Germany Heglioland in exchange for Zanzibar and Pemba.

1904
Entente Cordiale settles British and French disputes over Morocco, Egypt, Madagascar, and the Suez Canal; France creates federal structure for its Africa empire at Dakar.

Northern Africa

The British and French ruled most of northern Africa, with the Italians controlling parts of Libya and Eritrea and the Spanish parts of what is now Morocco. The French invaded Algeria in 1830–31 and gradually spread until they controlled most of West Africa. The British made Egypt a protectorate in 1882 then spread south into Sudan. Rivalry between the two colonial powers came to a head in 1898 at Foshoda when British forces found the French flag flying over territories they regarded as their own. The French withdrew but the incident led to the *Entente Cordiale* of 1904 which calmed French and British disputes in Africa.

Top: Traditional costumes of people in Algeria in the 1880s.

Left: This Yoruba statue from West Africa shows a Catholic missionary travelling on a donkey.

The raising of the French flag in Timbuktu (modern Mali), in 1894.

Missionaries and Religion

There were Christian missionaries all over Africa throughout the 19th century. They were especially important in opposing and helping to end the slave trade. Many people in northern Africa were Muslim while others maintained traditional beliefs. Opposition to the colonial powers sometimes coalesced into religious opposition too, for example when Muhammad Ahmed (the Mahdi) rebelled against Anglo-Egyptian rule and founded a strict Islamic state in Sudan.

Right: Behanzin, the king of Dahomey (modern Benin). The French had a trade agreement with Dahomey, but war broke out in 1892 and the kingdom became part of French West Africa.

Imperial Power

The colonial powers roughly imposed Western ways and methods of trade and taxation. They abolished local currencies, replacing them with European coinage. To pay the new taxes, many Africans became wage laborers on the large sugar, cocoa, and rubber estates that sprang up, worked in the mines, or helped build infrastructure, such as the railroads. Many aspects of the local cultures were destroyed and the people were resentful and looking for ways to revolt.

Above: The Suez Canal was a vital shipping route for Britain as it greatly shortened the sea journey to its colonies in India, Australia and New Zealand.

Above: European tourists in front of the Sphinx at Giza, Egypt.

Right: A European woman meets local women in Algiers.

Egypt and the Suez Canal

The Suez Canal, opened in 1869, was largely financed by the French and had been designed and built by a Frenchman (Ferdinand de Lesseps). But when the Egyptian ruler had financial difficulties in 1875 he sold most of his shares to the British government. In 1879 the Egyptian ruler refused to honor his foreign debt and Britain and France forced him to abdicate. Despite rebellion, Britain then took control of Egypt and slowly moved its sphere of influence south through the Sudan and British East Africa.

Below: Leopold II (1835–1909) greatly expanded the Belgian presence in Africa. He made a fortune from rubber and ivory.

The Belgian Congo

In 1879–84 King Leopold II of Belgium hired Henry Morton Stanley, who had extensively explored the Congo River region, to set up Belgian outposts along the river. In 1885 the region became Leopold's personal colony, named Congo Free State. The king's harsh rule brought protests, however, and the Belgian government took control in 1908, renaming the colony the Belgian Congo.

Left: A French soldier plants the tricolor in Madagascar.

Other Colonial Powers in Southern Africa

France claimed the island of Madagascar and the Portuguese ruled over Angola and Mozambique. Germany had control of German South West Africa. German settlers were encouraged to settle on land belonging to the Herero and Nama tribes. In 1903–04 the Herero and Nama people rebelled against the colony. Their rebellion was brutally put down; more than 80 percent of the Herero lost their lives.

SOUTHERN AFRICA

1814
Britain acquires the cape Colony.

1820
20,00 new British settlers arrive at the Cape Colony.

1834
Britain abolishes slavery in its empire.

1835–37
Boers make the Great Trek north to Natal.

1843
Britain annexes Natal.

1852–54
Britain recognizes independence of Transvaal and Orange Free State.

1871
Diamonds found at Kimberley.

1877–78
British annex Transvaal.

1881
First Boer War.

1886
Gold found in Transvaal.

1889–1902
Second Boer War.

1910
Union of South Africa formed.

Southern Africa

In 1800 there were already 15,000 Boer (Afrikaans or Dutch) farmers living in the Cape Colony. Britain annexed the region early in the 19th century and subsequent friction with the Boers caused many to emigrate north in the Great Trek (see page 39). In 1843 the British annexed Natal and the Boers moved further north again to form the Orange Free State and the Transvaal. When diamonds and gold were discovered there in the 1860s and 1880s, respectively, the British again annexed Boer territories. This led to the Boer Wars and the ultimate defeat of the Boers.

Left: Boers soldiers in the Second Boer War of 1899–1902.

The Boer Wars

Beginning in 1880, the British and the Boers (from the Dutch for "farmers") fought a series of wars for control of southern Africa. In the first Boer War (1881) the Boers rebelled against British rule and regained the Afrikaner state of Transvaal. In the second Boer War (1899–1902), the Boers were successful at first, besieging Ladysmith, Mafeking, and Kimberley. The British, under Lord Kitchener and Lord Roberts, brought in many more troops and finally defeated the Boers. The two Afrikaner states became British colonies.

Below: German colonial troops attacking the Herero people in 1904.

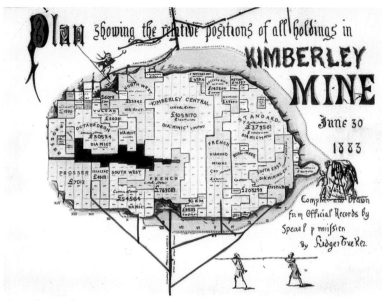

South African Gold

The gold rush in South Africa started in 1886 after gold was found in Witwatersrand. People from as far away as Britain and India poured into the Transvaal and the region quickly became the world's largest goldfield. Growth was spectacular, with new roads and railroads transforming the countryside, and foreign investment and expertise quickly creating a modern nation of the whole area. To protect their interests in the area the British annexed the Transvaal and invaded Zululand.

Below: A Zulu shield and spears. The Zulus developed a new kind of spear, called an assegai, that was not thrown at enemies in battle but used to stab them.

The Zulu People

The kingdom of the Zulus, a Bantu people, was formed in the early 19th century. The Zulus clashed with the Boers in 1838, and won a great battle at Isandlhwana against the British in 1879. They were finally defeated by the British at Ulundi. The Zulu king was exiled and former Zululand was divided into 13 chieftaincies. The end of the Zulu military threat encouraged the Boers to shake off British power in Transvaal and led to the first Boer War (1881).

Below: A Zulu village. Zulu society was well organized, with clearly defined roles for men and women. Women worked in the fields and carried out domestic chores, including the weaving of baskets. Zulu homes were dome-shaped and had spartan furnishings. Millet was a staple crop and it was ground into a flour then cooked into a thick porridge. Zulu men married quite late, when they were in their mid-30s, while women were usually 10 to 15 years younger. Some wealthy men had more than one wife.

Glossary

Annex To incorporate an area or region into another area or region, usually without asking permission.

Archipelago A chain or cluster of islands that was formed by the movement of ocean plates. Now used to refer to any island group or, sometimes, to a sea containing a large number of scattered islands.

Cartographer A person who makes maps.

Colonialism The extension of a nation's government beyond its borders. Colonial powers either send settlers to take over the colony, or set up a local government to exploit the indigenous people and their wealth.

Circumnavigate To travel all the way around a place, such as an island, a continent, or the Earth, by boat or ship.

Civil war Armed conflict between different groups of people from the same country.

Colony A country's overseas land or territory.

Diplomacy The art of managing international relations with other countries through negotiation rather than by warfare.

Dynasty A line of rulers coming from the same family, or a period during which they reign.

Economy The wealth and resources of a country or a region.

Emancipation A term used to describe various efforts to obtain political rights or equality. In the case of slavery, it meant when slaves gained their freedom.

Empire All of the land controlled by a ruler or government, including overseas territories.

Exploitation An ongoing social relationship in which certain persons are being mistreated or unfairly used for the benefit of others.

Heathen Like pagan, a term used to describe religions and spiritual practises of pre-Christian Europe, and also a derogatory (bad) term for non-Christian religious traditions or beliefs

Imperial power A term used to describe something that relates to an empire, emperor, or the concept of imperialism.

Imperialism A system of building foreign empires for military and trade advantages.

Indigenous people Term used to describe an ethnic group that has inhabited a given region for a long time, as compared to migrants who have populated the region more recently and who are usually greater in number.

Infrastructure The technical structures that support a society, such as roads, railroads, water supply, waste management systems, and so on.

Merchant fleet or navy A nation's commercial or trading ships and the crews that sail them.

Minister An important official who serves a ruler or in a government.

Missionary A follower of a religion who works to convert those who do not share the missionary's faith.

Monarchy A country in which the ruler is a king or queen who rules by right of birth rather than by being elected, for example.

Mutiny A conspiracy among members of a group (usually members of the military or the crew of a ship) to openly oppose or overthrow an existing authority. The term is commonly used for a rebellion among members of the military against their superior officers.

Noble A high-ranking person who is a member of the aristocracy. They may be noble by birth, or may be awarded their title.

Obsolete Something that is out of date or old fashioned and has been replaced by something better and more advanced.

Opium A narcotic, or drug, made from the sap of immature seed pods of opium poppies.

Parliament A formal gathering of people that debates and decides a country's laws. Members of parliament may be chosen by an election.

Philosophy The study of human thought about the meaning of life and the correct way to live.

Policy The course of action decided by a ruler, minister, government or parliament.

Prospector A person who explores an area for natural resources such as minerals such as gold or diamonds, or oil.

Uprising An organized attempt to oppose authority; a conflict in which one group tries to take control from another. Similar in meaning to rebellion.

Rebel To rise up and challenge a ruler or government, sometimes by force; also the name for a person who does this.

Reform To change an organization or system to make it work better or more efficiently.

Regent Someone who governs on behalf of a young prince or princess who inherits the throne before they are old enough officially to become the next king or queen.

Republic A country in which the ruler is elected and is not a monarch who rules by birthright.

Revolution A change in power or government which occurs in a short period of time, often as a result of violents protests and struggle.

Secular Something that is not religious, for example a government, country, organization, festival, or building.

Sepoy A native of India who was a soldier allied to a European power, usually the Britain. Specifically, it was the term used in the British Indian Army for an infantry private.

Siege The surrounding of a city or fort by the army of their enemy in an attempt to capture it. A siege can last many days with the intention of starving the people inside so that they will surrender.

Subject A person who lives under the rule of a king or queen.

Tax Money people must pay to a government, church or ruler to help support them or a particular cause.

Treaty A written agreement between two or more countries or rulers, often drawn up to end a war.

Index